The New York Times

POCKET MBA SERIES

BUSINESS FINANCING

25 KEYS TO RAISING MONEY

DILEEP RAO, PH.D.
RICHARD CARDOZO, PH.D.
University of Minnesota

Lebhar-Friedman Books
NEW YORK • CHICAGO • LOS ANGELES • LONDON • PARIS • TOKYO

For *The New York Times*
Mike Levitas, Editorial Director, Book Development
Tom Redburn, General Series Editor
Brent Bowers, Series Editor
James Schembari, Series Editor

Lebhar-Friedman Books
425 Park Avenue
New York, NY 10022

Published by Lebhar-Friedman Books
Lebhar-Friedman Books is a company of Lebhar-Friedman Inc.

Printed in the United States of America

Library of Congress Cataloging-in-Publication Data
Rao, Dileep.
    Business financing : 25 keys to raising money / Dileep Rao.
      p. cm.—(The New York Times pocket MBA series ; vol. 3)
    Includes index.
    ISBN 0-86730-770-6 (paperback)
    1. Business enterprises—Finance. I. Title. II. Series.
    HG4026 .R357 1999
    658.15—dc21   99-27690
                                          CIP

DESIGN & PRODUCTION BY MILLER WILLIAMS DESIGN ASSOCIATES

Visit our Web site at lfbooks.com

INTRODUCTION

LEBHAR-FRIEDMAN BOOKS is proud to present *The New York Times* Pocket MBA Series, 12 invaluable reference volumes that are easily accessible to all businesspersons, from first level managers to the executive suite. The books are written by Ph.D.s who teach in the MBA programs in some of the finest schools in the country. A team of business editors from *The New York Times*—Mike Levitas, Tom Redburn, Brent Bowers, and James Schembari—provided their own expertise to edit a reference series that is beyond compare.

The New York Times Pocket MBA Series offers quick-reference key points learned in top MBA programs. The 25-key structure of each volume presents an unparalleled synopsis of crucial principles of specific areas of business expertise. The unique approach to this series packages academic books for consumers in an easy-to-use trade format that is ideal for the individual businessperson as well as an excellent training reference manual. Be sure to get all 12 titles in the series to complete your own MBA education.

Joseph Mills
Senior Managing Editor
Lebhar-Friedman Books

The New York Times Pocket MBA
Series includes these 12 volumes:

Analyzing Financial Statements

Business Planning

Business Financing

Growing & Managing a Business

Organizing a Company

Forecasting Budgets

Tracking & Controlling Costs

Sales & Marketing

Managing Investment

Going Global

Leadership & Vision

The Board of Directors

25 KEYS TO RAISING MONEY

C O N T E N T S

KEY 1

Plan ahead

This may sound obvious, but a surprising number of entrepreneurs wait until the last moment to seek financing. By then, their desperation shows through—making potential lenders leery.

The fact that a company needs money urgently makes no difference whatsoever to financial institutions or investors. What they do care about is the credibility of the company's business plan and the character and commitment of its managers. And they will take their time doing what they call their "due diligence," which basically means calling around to check on your background and evaluating financial viability.

The length of time required to evaluate and approve a loan or investment varies from source to source. In general, this period is shorter if the risk is lower or if an established relationship exists with the borrower. Government agencies, such as the Federal Small Business Administration, tend to take longer than commercial lenders with the paperwork, but their terms are generally more attractive and well worth the wait.

A general rule of thumb is to get the financing wheels in motion at least six months before you actually will need the money. Planning ahead like this will give you the luxury of meeting and evaluating a broad range of financiers to find out if you fit their criteria and, if you do, to choose among their offers.

There is a right way and a wrong way to make contact. The wrong way is the cold call: "Hi, my name is Sarah and I'd like some of your money." The right way is an introduction from a financial professional that the financier is sure to respect, such as an accountant, an attorney, a financial consultant or another entrepreneur. Investors often receive thousands of business plans over the course of their careers, but meet with fewer than 20 percent of the people who pitch them. The surest way to count yourself among the elite fifth is to get a personal introduction.

What if you don't need financing in the foreseeable future? Our advice is the same: Plan ahead; better yet, plan way ahead. Developing positive relationships with potential financiers should be an ongoing process; you never know when you'll suddenly be short of cash.

Having the right management team in place is crucial. Financiers like to work with companies whose management is experienced in the industry, who have had high-level responsibility in their previous jobs and who have a solid track record of success. No matter how dazzling your business plan or how promising your product, they will balk at thought of "training" your management with their money.

Venture capitalists prefer to invest in businesses that are managed by a team rather than an individual. They are even happier if the team has worked together successfully in the past.

If you do not have the sort of training financiers look for, you should immediately:

◆ go and get it; or

◆ find a partner who does have it.

One last tip: You won't get very far with financiers if you haven't made a serious financial commitment to your business. Are you willing to risk most or all of your net worth to see your venture through? Are you willing to take a pay cut from your previous salary until it becomes profitable? You had better be; financiers expect you to share in the pain for the promised gain.

KEY 2

Know how much cash you'll need, when you'll need it and how you'll use it

Those are the first three questions any financier will ask you, and you need to have specific, detailed answers to show your credibility. The information can help you, too, by pointing you in the right direction in your search for financing. For example, many financial institutions have minimum and maximum limits on lending to any one business, and borrowers may choose to avoid a particular source because the amount of funding is small when compared with the level of paperwork needed.

In calculating how much you need, you should follow one cardinal principle: Be totally honest in all your projections, whether they be for your expenses, your revenue or your market share. You should acknowledge the hard fact that some of your customers will be a few days or even a few weeks late in paying their bills, for example, Likewise, you should give a realistic assessment of how quickly you will be able to pay your suppliers. As for taxes and wages, these must be paid on time; there is no wiggle room, so don't try to create any.

To get the size of the loan you are requesting right:

- Evaluate the assumptions used to make the projections and make sure they are realistic.

- Find the right time horizon. You obviously don't want to have to keep going back to financiers every few months. On the other hand, you shouldn't borrow so much money from venture capitalists that you end up with a negligible stake in your company.

- Do not add excessive "cushions" of cash to your calculation of what you actually will need. Many financiers assume that entrepreneurs will spend all the money available to them and will balk at giving you too much of a margin for error. In fact, if you make a request for a disproportionate cushion they might be less inclined to do a deal with you. On the other hand, you should create some sort of cushion to absorb unexpected expenses. Otherwise, you'll be making a return trip to your financier sooner than you think, and the greeting you get may not be the friendliest in the world.

- If your business isn't a startup, make sure your projections conform to its history and management record and that it take into account current market conditions such as orders on hand and the number and size of your competitors. In other words, show your financiers where the company has been and where it expects to go.

If a little money does not go,

much money can not come.

Chinese and Japanese saying

Many conservative financiers (such as bankers) will only fund companies with strong historical statements. Venture capitalists are more concerned about projections for revenue and profit growth because only by meeting or exceeding them will they achieve their targeted returns. Weaker, or new, companies are not likely to get very far with either banks or venture capitalists and will probably have to look for Government financing.

This brings us to the final question: How will you use the money you raise? Lenders will want to know how much you plan to invest in real estate and easily resold facilities and equipment; how much in specialized facilities and equipment and how much in working capital and executive salaries. They are more likely to lend money for the first categories, and may require that specialized equipment and all or a portion of working capital be financed by raising equities. Most financiers will require that executives' cash compensation be held to a minimum until the business proves its viability.

Here are answers to some key questions often asked by entrepreneurs:

◆ How far into the future should I make projections? It depends on your financing source. Most commonly, lenders will ask you to look ahead either for one year, two years or five years. And investors want to know how much you need for each stage.

◆ Will I be making monthly, quarterly or annual statements to my lenders? Usually, they will expect to see monthly statements for the first year, and monthly statements thereafter until your company goes into the black. Once it does, many lenders will require quarterly statements during the first year of profitability and annual statements after that.

◆ Which statements will lenders expect me to provide? The key documents are the balance sheet, the income statement and the cash-flow statement. For many businesses, of course, the actual level of cash and hence the cash-flow statement is the most important because that can influence survival.

◆ Who should do the projections? You or your management should do them because it is your business. You can have your outside accountants check them for accuracy, if needed. If you delegate this task to your outside accountant, make sure you know enough that you can answer questions when asked. And make sure you know enough about your statements and projections that you know when you have missed your projections and need to make changes.

KEY 3

Identify the events and forces that could affect the amount and timing of your needs for cash, and how they might do so

Nothing ever goes completely according to plan. You need to know what circumstances might affect your need for cash, and how to cope with changed circumstances.

Symptoms of changes in cash needs include higher or lower sales than forecast, higher or lower costs and faster or slower payments. To find the causes behind these symptoms—so you'll know what actions to take—examine the identity and number of your customers, how much each purchases, the average price received for your product or service, unforeseen expenditures, longer (or shorter) times for research projects, competitors' behavior, changes in technology, legal or regulatory actions involving your company—in short, all the factors that determine your need for cash.

Now comes the hard part: Decide which of these factors will have the greatest impact on the amount and timing of your needs for cash.

Classify these factors as (1) cannot be forecast, (2) can be forecast but not managed, and (3) can be forecast and managed at least in part. For the first, plan a cushion; for the second, a cushion and a contingency plan; for the third, a contingency plan.

A "cushion" is a reserve of cash or a commitment by a lender to provide cash in case you need it. It's easiest to get a cushion from a lender if you have collateral, or from an equity investor if you have a history of growth and of making reasonably accurate forecasts. Get the cushion if you can, but don't dilute your interest excessively or pledge so much in collateral or covenants (restrictions that accompany a loan) that it constrains your ability to grow or limits your options to adapt to changes.

Try to avoid covenants that tie up all your assets or options to raise more money in the future when needed. If all assets are tied up, negotiate a commitment from lenders to release some of them if benchmarks in such areas as sales, profits, net worth and outstanding loans are met. If that doesn't work, you can always solve the problem by paying off your current lenders and finding new ones. But it is not as simple to buy back shares or equity interests.

Contingency plans will specify what to do if foreseeable but unwelcome events occur. Be prepared to tell a financier what you'll do in response to a sudden shrinkage in demand, to cost overruns, to competitive pressures and to other events that could affect cash flow.

Build flexibility into your forecasts and financing plans. Choose financiers who understand your industry and business. They'll know what factors are likely to put your plan off-track, and will recognize normal variations from your plan, which will not alarm them.

Honesty, honesty, honesty: In the end, that is the intangible that financiers value most. For example, sometimes you will know in the thick of negotiations for one loan that you will soon be asking for another loan. Let your financiers know you'll probably be returning for more funds, and when.

Wall Street has only two emotions: fear and greed.

Bill McGowan

KEY 4

Where should you look for money?

Seek money from the right source. Because of the specialization of the financial markets in the United States in recent years, most institutions provide only limited types of financing. Approaching the wrong type of financial institution for any type of financing is a waste of time and effort.

Most financial institutions have criteria for lending or investing, taking into consideration such factors as a company's size, the stage of its growth and its potential for further expansion, its location, the industry that it is in and its financial strength. Many also limit the size of loans or investments to any one company.

You should negotiate hard for the best possible financing terms, of course, but you should also shop around for something less tangible—good vibes. Finding a financier who is actually interested in your business and who makes an effort to understand how it works is more important than you might think. For one thing, such attention to detail augurs well for the establishment of a long-range relationship. For another, it means that financiers are likely to support your business a little longer and provide a little more help even if you fail to reach your initial projections.

The financial world is broadly categorized into lenders, investors and development financiers. Lenders lend money—debt, in their parlance—for a specified period at a given interest rate. They expect regular payments of principal and interest. Investors buy equity—a share of ownership in the business. They typically expect to get their original investment and return on it back through sale of stock at a later date. Development financiers, usually Federal, state or local agencies with a mandate to promote certain forms of economic activity, may offer debt, equity or a combination of the two.

From the point of view of the entrepreneur, the cost of the money depends on the perceived risk to the financier. Debt costs less than equity.

Bankers are normally risk averse because they do not charge enough to compensate for high risk. The spread between their cost of money and the rates they charge is usually under 400 basis points (4 percent). Bankers usually lend on the basis of the company's historical and projected cash flow, debt service capability, guarantees and collateral. They want a secondary source of repayment of their principal and interest if the first one—cash flow—does not materialize.

Venture capitalists, essentially investors who put their money in startups and emerging businesses, and so-called angels, rich individuals who do the same thing, are hard bargainers. If they like your

Money often costs too much.

Ralph Waldo Emerson, Wealth

company—and they only like a small number of the enterprises they look at—they will demand a big chunk of the equity in return for their capital. But they have no choice; so many companies that they add to their portfolios either falter or fail that they have to offset that risk by the hope of huge returns on their successful investments.

In essence, these venture capitalists take a share of a company's profits in the form of stock, and the annualized, compounded cost of their money to entrepreneurs runs at around 20 percent, and can go as high as 100 percent for companies in the research and development stage.

Development financial institutions generally administer programs that offer higher-risk financing at below-market rates. If you want cheaper financing, this is where you should go.

Many businesses avoid these sources because private financiers have scared them away with horror stories about the paperwork. However, the forms aren't really all that daunting, and you can always pay a specialist to fill them out for you.

These development-finance sources offer cheaper financing for the purpose of achieving social benefits like creating jobs, promoting exports, developing new technologies, assisting minority citizens and spurring moribund local economies. If your business offers any of these benefits, check out these sources. Who knows—someone might even give you a grant.

Explore all the alternatives. The American financial system is the richest and most diverse in the world. Mine it for all it is worth.

KEY 5

Match your needs, returns and risks with financiers' capacity, goals and risk preferences

To make your financing search easier, you need to match the financing sources to your needs. Financiers have different capacities to finance and absorb risks. And there are two levels of criteria you should examine.

The first level is among different types of institutions. As an example, individual investors can be classified into categories based on their risk-assumption capacity. Family and friends assume the most, often followed by "affiliated angels," such as suppliers and vendors, who not only know the industry but also stand to gain directly, and by "industry angels," or corporate executives who know the industry and can evaluate a new technology or concept better than financial angels and have the money to assume risks. (Financial angels are basically rich people who invest in startups.)

Banks do not provide risk financing. They do not charge sufficiently to take the risk of loss of principal (amount loaned or invested). That is why venture capitalists exist. It is their business to invest in high-risk ventures—in order to seek high returns.

After choosing the right type of financial source, you then should choose the right financier—that is, someone with experience and contacts and whose personality is compatible with yours.

As you go about your search, here are some ground rules to bear in mind:

◆ If you are seeking debt financing, borrow against fixed assets like equipment and real estate, rather than against working capital, especially because there are a number of government programs to finance fixed assets, and they are usually cheaper.

◆ Use your equity and for working capital.

◆ Finance short-term assets, such as working capital, with short-term debt, such as line of credit, and finance long-term assets, such as real estate, with long-term debt. Short-term debt should never be used to acquire long-term fixed assets.

◆ It is nearly impossible to raise debt financing to pay for losses; selling a stake in your venture is about the only way to get money for that purpose.

Seek harmony of interests. Raising money is the not the destination, just the means to get there. The destination should be a profitable and growing business. To achieve this, you need to be aware of issues that can affect ongoing relationships, such as the possibility that a bank will demand repayment of the loan at the most inopportune time. You can reduce this risk by seeking a harmony of interests with the financier.

If there is a harmony of interests between the company and the investing or lending institution, raising money becomes easier. And the ongoing relationship is also more successful. Therefore, determine the financier's interests and history, and see if there is a good fit.

When there is harmony of interests, financiers don't turn tail and run at the slightest hint of problems like those banks that expand into an industry or an area because it was the "in" thing to do. For examples of this kind of activity, look at banks that exited from China not so long ago. China was a hot area in the early 1990's. Then, in 1999, it turned cooler and many banks stopped lending or bailed out.

KEY 6

Friends and family: why you should stay in touch, what they can do for you and why they might do it

I f you have no track record, friends and family members are often the only ones who will invest in your venture. Their money will enable you to prove yourself to other investors.

Often, friends and family will accept a valuation of the company that you could never sell to others. In fact, as so often happens, you might have to go back to them later on to inform them that you are negotiating with professional investors who put a much lower price tag on your firm.

At that point, you might have to offer your friends and relatives a compensatory carrot, such as additional stock, and confess that you did not know what you were doing when you put an unrealistic value on the enterprise.

In any case, you had better take the professionals' estimates seriously. After all, they are experienced in gauging risk, and know that a large number of

**Every man has enough
power left to carry out that
of which he is convinced.**

Johann Wolfgang Von Goethe

new ventures stumble. If you refuse to budge, they will probably refuse to open their pocketbooks.

By contrast, friends and family members are often unsophisticated in their financial understanding, and may have a blind faith that you will succeed. Typically, they will say something like, "If you can pay the same return on my money as I am currently getting" on, say, United States Treasury bonds, "I will be happy." Such thinking betrays their naivete; in essence, they are declaring that you have the same creditworthiness as the Federal government. Now, how true is that?

Why would friends and relatives finance your

venture? The answer is obvious, isn't it? They have faith in you, and, perhaps even more, they want to help you succeed.

But should you accept their financing? Many entrepreneurs do not want to turn to people so close to them, in the understandable fear that they might damage their relationship, perhaps irreparably, if things go wrong. On the other hand, if nobody else is putting up the money you need, family members and friends might be your only recourse.

Our advice: Take the plunge. Be honest about the potential risk, and don't lean too heavily on someone who shows great reluctance to dig into his pockets. Moreover, you obviously don't want to jeopardize Aunt Bertha's retirement nest egg or the cash hoard that your friend Billy plans to use as a down payment on his dream house.

Otherwise, look at it this way:

If you take their money and make a killing, they will love you. If you don't take their money, you'll come out a loser no matter what happens; that is, if your business thrives, they will resent you, and if it fails, you'll be so miserable it won't matter what they think.

So why not take the money? Why did they become your friends or family in the first place if not to help you in your time of need?

What's the best way to obtain their financing?

It depends on how much risk you want them to take, what type of financing is most needed by your venture, and whether or not you want to pay interest. Among the more common options to obtain financing from friends and family are common stock, or equity, and subordinated debt with equity features. (Key 13 describes both in more detail.)

KEY 7

Lenders come in many forms. Find the one that's right for you

Know the different types of institutions that lend money, including suppliers, leasing companies and others. Understand how lenders expect to be repaid, and how they reduce risk. Some of the key types of lenders for emerging businesses include:

◆ Commercial banks, the department stores of lending. They do all types of loans, but they don't take risks and they can't spend large amounts of time with any single customer.

◆ Commercial finance companies. They provide working capital to companies that are experiencing growth in inventory and accounts receivable and are thus either losing money or showing flab in their balance sheet. These borrowers are usually referred to the finance companies by banks that don't want to deal with financially weak businesses. They charge more for their money, but are more flexible with their financing and monitor their loans closely, in effect providing a "free" consulting service. In fact, after they do their due diligence, they sometimes know more about the financial aspects of the company than the entrepreneur does.

◆ Leasing companies. They finance equipment by renting it out for a fixed period of time. Since they own the asset, they can repossess it if payments are missed, costing the customer money and creating delays in production. This gives them greater leverage than commercial banks, which have to go through foreclosure to obtain their collateral, and makes them more disposed than banks to finance a large portion of your equipment.

◆ Suppliers. They are key, primary sources of credit. Make sure that you have a good credit rating and that suppliers are aware of it, since the cost of credit is built into their pricing.

Do not, under any circumstances, use the tax collector as your lender. Resist the temptation to postpone payment of your payroll taxes just because the Internal Revenue Service isn't breathing down your neck. The penalties can be extremely onerous.

Lenders expect to be repaid through the cash flow of the business. Because making mistakes can kill their careers, they will question you closely about your historical cash flow and your projected cash flow. If you have no cash flow to repay the loan (at least the interest for the first year), you need to raise equity.

And bankers always seek a secondary source of repayment of their debt in case the primary one—cash flow—fails to materialize. Thus they seek collateral or guarantees from persons or institutions with the means to repay the loan.

Collateral can include inventory, accounts receivable, equipment, real estate, stocks and bonds and savings accounts, in short, anything of value that could be sold to pay back the loan.

When a company has insufficient collateral to justify the loan it is seeking, lenders often suggest that the owners and officers raise additional capital using their personal assets, such as second mortgages on their homes, as collateral. Moreover, lenders generally require owners and officers to co-sign loans.

In seeking a loan, you should be familiar with a calculation known as the loan-to-value-of-collateral ratio, or more simply loan-to-value ratio, that lenders use to determine how wide to open the financial spigot. Here are some common loan-to-value ratios:

♦ For inventory: Generally, they will lend between 25 percent and 50 percent of the value of finished goods but will lend up to 80 percent of the value of certain commodities. If the goods are unfinished, though, forget it; the ratio is zero percent.

♦ Accounts receivable: up to 80 percent if the billing terms are reasonable, the customers are credit-worthy and the accounts are current. Overdue accounts are usually eliminated from consideration.

♦ Equipment: up to 75 percent, depending on

how easy it would be to sell it, and up to 100 percent for leases. Some government programs, such as those run by the Small Business Administration, will lend up to 90 percent.

◆ Real estate: up to 75 percent for most general-purpose real estate, depending on cash flow; some government programs will lend up to 90 percent.

You should also know about cash-flow ratios. The two main ones are called:

◆ Times interest earned, or the ratio of your projected earnings to your interest-payment obligations.

◆ Fixed charges coverage, or the ratio of cash available for payment of principal and interest to your principal and interest.

KEY 8

Explore a broad range of alternatives to understand where to seek financing

Entrepreneurs usually overlook some very attractive sources of financing because they fail to spend the time and energy to find out what's available. Typically, they'll talk to one or two people, perhaps their Uncle Charlie or Cousin Mary who started a business, and to their local banker. That's a mistake. You should explore every option—even if it is a long shot.

Venture capitalists turn down 98 percent or more of the companies that contact them. To get financing from them, you need to know what they seek. Obviously, it would make no sense to approach a firm that specializes in biotechnology startups if you are a software company.

Two good reference guides to help you in your search are the *Directory of Small Business Investment Companies* issued by the Small Business Administration (www.sba.gov) and the *Venture Capital Directory* published by the National Venture Capital Association (www.nvca.com) You can also check out the web page of PricewaterhouseCoopers (www.pwc-global.com) for a list of active venture capitalists and their latest investments.

In general, venture capitalists seek to invest in high-growth ventures that provide the expectation of extremely high annual compounded returns to balance the risk that they assume. These projections can range from 20 percent in mature, high-growth ventures already showing sales and profits to 60 percent or more for startups.

Venture capitalists seek to invest large amounts—usually a minimum of $1 million and up—in enterprises that have experienced management teams. Sometimes, if they have a high opinion of the technology and business concept, they will find the right management team to complement the developers of the technology.

For smaller amounts, many new ventures go to friends and family, and to professional individual investors called angels. Angels can specialize in high growth ventures in their area or in their industry. Your accountant or attorney may know of such angels and help you contact them.

Lenders reject requests for financing for all sorts of reasons, from concern about a company's lack of history or profits to worries about its prospects to lack of confidence in its management. But not all bankers think alike; if one turns you down, try another.

Bankers prefer to lend to firms whose projected cash flow will repay the loan, which have adequate collateral to satisfy the loan if cash flow fails, and whose principals—the entrepreneurs—will commit their personal assets to guarantee the loan. But some bankers, particularly smaller or newer banks, are more aggressive and willing to take a chance on you even if all the numbers aren't perfect. They hope to grow with you.

Many entrepreneurs start spending money before they get it because they think that the bankers have made a commitment. Alas, a banker's comment that "everything looks good; all we need now is the committee's approval" is not the same thing as receiving a check in the mail. Until you have the money in the bank, don't spend it.

Loss of money is bewailed

with louder lamentations

than a death.

Juvenal, Satires

KEY 9

Getting development financing: understand what's available and what each seeks

One of the ironies of financing is that its cost is highest for those who can least afford it. Risk influences the cost of money, and risk is generally assumed to be highest in the smallest firms.

The good news for such firms is that one type of lender flouts the law of financing that return should balance risk: development-finance institutions.

These institutions represent one of the prime, and often most underutilized, sources of business financing. In most areas there are at least 16 sources of local-development sources, at least seven types of state development sources and at least 15 types of federal financing sources. (Note that not all areas will have all types of local and state sources.)

How do you find development finance sources? Call your local Chamber of Commerce, local economic-development organization, state economic-development organization or the grand-daddy of them all, the Federal Small Business Administration. And these are just a few of the opportunities. (You can also check our "Financing Business: How to do it right!" by Dileep Rao. (Interfinance Corporation, 1999.)

Often, bankers try to discourage the customers from seeking development financing because of the supposed "excessive" paperwork involved, but that criticism is often unfounded. Sure, there are extra forms, but you'll probably have the requested information in your business plan. And the benefits are well worth the time you spend filling them out: cash you need at below-market interest rates and other favorable terms.

What's in it for the lenders? Plenty. Remember, they are Government agencies or non-profit corporations whose goal is to fulfill social policy goals like:

◆ job creation, especially in low-income areas;

◆ minority business development;

◆ technology development;

◆ promoting access to world markets, since the United States gains jobs and an improved trade balance when exports increase;

◆ small business development, a goal for all levels of Government because it is viewed as a way to create jobs and spark innovation.

Development-financing sources are not supposed

to compete with the private sector and to avoid doing so, many include a "but for" clause in their contracts stating, "But for this financing, this project would not take place." This means that you cannot, in the interest of speedy access to cash, borrow from a private lender and then try to repay the loan with financing from lower-cost development finance.

Lately, however, many local and state development-finance sources are moving away from this clause to encourage economic growth and to retain industry.

KEY 10

Use the right process to raise financing for your business. What sounds easy may be the most difficult

There are many different ways to raise money for your business, and even more state and federal laws dealing with the process. If you are raising money from non-institutional financiers, you should get legal advice from an experienced securities lawyer.

The various processes for raising money include:

◆ Direct private placements of debt with financial institutions, such as banks, commercial-finance companies, leasing companies and venture-capital companies. This is by far the most common method. To do this, you don't need any legal documents, nor do you need a lawyer, though you might feel more comfortable hiring one to make sure that you are doing everything right. The procedure is simple: You approach the financial institution and provide it with the information it asks for, most of which can be found in your business plan, plus details about your history and financial worth.

◆ Indirect private placements by institutions, such as insurance companies, through investment bankers. These institutions will only consider financing companies that are recommended to them by the investment bankers whose judgement they value. Normally, these placements are for debt, but sometimes they are for equity if the company plans an initial public offering, or is a candidate for a merger, soon.

◆ Private placements of equity by individuals. These transactions can be handled by the company itself or through an investment banker. This method of financing normally is done by emerging, high-growth ventures that do not have a long history and are seeking equity. A hodgepodge of state and Federal laws govern such offerings, so don't go this route without an attorney. First, check the attorney's expertise and ask tough questions about his fees; these have become negotiable.

◆ Initial public offerings. I.P.O.'s are probably the toughest form of financing and can cost more than $500,000, so it is usually high-growth companies that attempt them. Investment bankers usually handle these transactions, and they can do so on an "underwritten" basis, where they are obligated to buy the stock and find buyers, or on a "best efforts" basis, where they buy the stock only if they find enough investors to sell it to.

◆ In recent years, a new form of I.P.O. called

the Direct Public Offering, or D.P.O., has become popular in states that have created so-called Small Corporate Offering Registration programs. Aimed at small companies, S.C.O.R. programs are cheaper than ordinary I.P.O.'s, have much-simplified paperwork and allow the entrepreneurs to sell stock themselves, rather than through an investment banker. But you should definitely consult an experienced attorney. And never forget the adage that what sounds easy may be the most difficult.

For example, selling your own stock to the public may sound easy, but many D.P.O.'s fail because the other party to the transaction—the buyer—doesn't materialize.

In most cases, development financiers offer the cheapest form of financing. But they also take the longest time to approve the financing. Companies in a hurry miss out on these great deals. Therefore plan early—at least six months before you actually need to get your hands on the cash. Take advantage of the inverse relationship between the cost of money and the time needed to raise it!

KEY 11

Match investors to the appropriate investment instruments

Investors have different appetites for risk. Risk can be influenced by the stage of the venture, the competitive advantage and proprietary technology, the expertise and experience of management and many other factors that can determine whether a venture succeeds, fails or lingers on but never reaches its potential.

One way to nudge investors to shift from the "no" or "maybe" column to an enthusiastic "yes" column might be to propose an instrument that will help them overcome their fear of losing money. The fact is, it is possible for a venture to fail and for financiers nevertheless to get their money back.

A simple example of this is the strategy used by asset-based lenders. These "risk-taking" lenders enter the scene when banks balk. Banks want businesses to have sufficient cash flow to be able to repay their loan and interest. They also insist on a secondary source of repayment, whether in the form of collateral that they can liquidate or guarantees from sources who could repay the loan.

Asset-based lenders do lend money to a business even when it does not have cash flow. They rely on their security in the form of collateral, and they closely monitor the loan, which banks are usually not qualified to do, to ensure that their collateral is sufficient to repay their loan. And they charge about 6 to 8 percentage points more than commercial banks for their efforts and risks taken.

Similarly, if investors are reluctant to put money in a venture because they don't know if there is a market for the common stock they are asked to buy, entrepreneurs can consider selling preferred stock with an agreement to redeem the stock after a certain time period. Or they can use subordinated convertible debt. This type of instrument allows the investors to have a secured position senior to all unsecured creditors, which includes trade creditors. (This means that they get paid after the senior lenders—banks—get their money.)

Some financial instruments in ascending order of risk include:

1 Senior loans across all assets: These are good for banks because they prefer the least risk.

2 Senior loans with specific named assets: These are good for vendors of equipment or asset-based lenders who are very specific in their needs.

3 Subordinated loans across all assets: These are good for smaller and community development venture capitalists, who often have a lower appetite for risk than the venture capital limited partnerships.

4 Unsecured loans: These are good for those who trust you and would like to help you succeed—usually friends and family who are not seeking a high return.

5 Preferred stock: This is for sophisticated investors who know that it adds equity to the venture while giving them the control they want.

6 Common stock: For friends, family and relatively unsophisticated angels who invest small amounts of money in high risk ventures.

In addition, if you are a new venture and don't expect to make any profits soon (and thus won't be paying any taxes), you might want to find instruments that offer tax benefits to investors.

KEY 12

Understand business stages, the cost of each stage, and its impact on dilution

Match financing sources to your stage and history. Financiers classify businesses on the basis of where they are on the development cycle.

Some key stages are:

◆ The research-and-development stage, when the business does not even have a product or service and has to develop it. In general, even among venture capitalists, only a small number consider investing at this stage and those who do invest expect to receive annual, compounded returns exceeding 60 percent.

◆ The seed stage, when the business has a product but very little else. It may not have a management team, suppliers, a place to operate or even a business plan. At this stage, the risks in the business are lower than those at the research-and-development stage, but investors still expect to see annual returns exceeding 50 percent.

- The startup stage, in which all the components except financing are in place. Investors look for returns exceeding 50 percent.

- The early-sales stage, when the venture has sales but is still unprofitable. Many of the risks have been eliminated, especially the questions of who will buy and at what price. However, since customers are still not buying in sufficient quantities to make a profit, the risks are higher than those acceptable to banks, and investors may require annual returns of 30 percent or more.

- The viability stage, when business has passed the break-even point, but lacks the size or track record to command a high price for its stock. Investors expect minimum returns from 20 to 30 percent per year.

- The pre-I.P.O. stage, when the venture has reached profitability and is close to having an initial public offering. (This was the normal route before the Internet craze has allowed companies to go public even before they have sales.) Since the I.P.O. is imminent, investors are usually seeking annual returns of 20 percent or more.

Due to the risks involved, new companies are less likely to attract debt (all other things being equal) because of their greater risk of failure. And a company with a history of losses or large variations in earnings will be less likely to attract debt than a company with a steady history of sales, earnings and growth. Stability or steady growth in sales and profits mean lower risks for financiers, and lower costs for the business.

For those who have difficulty raising capital in early stages, solutions include:

♦ Seeking financial institutions that work with, and perhaps specialize in, startups;

♦ Exploring the use of Government and development-financing programs, notably those offered by the Federal Small Business Administration, such as the so-called 7(a) guarantees that cover up to 80 percent of a bank loan and the "micro-loans" of up to $25,000 for small firms. Such programs usually assume more risk and offer lower interest rates than private investors do.

KEY 13

Select the right financial instruments to achieve your goals

There are a number of financial instruments, each with its own use, cost and term of repayment. Find the ones that are right for you and use them.

There are two broad groups of resources: debt and equity.

Equity instruments include common stock and preferred stock.

Common stockholders are the owners of the corporation and the stock certificates they own represent ownership. Unless the rights are given away in debt or investment agreements, shareholders owning over 50 percent of the outstanding shares of the corporation can control the assets and future of the corporation.

Preferred stockholders are usually institutional venture capitalists, such as the large-venture capital limited partnerships. Preferred stock has preference over common stock for dividends and for assets upon liquidation. Venture capitalists use preferred stock because it allows them to obtain greater rights than that of other common stock-holding minority shareholders, who possess few rights.

Debt instruments can be classified on the basis of term or collateral and security position.

On the basis of term, debt can be classified as short-, mid- or long-term:

- ◆ Short-term debt is repayable within one year and is used for short-term needs, such as regular trade credit or seasonal expenses.

- ◆ Mid-term debt, repayable over one to 10 years, is used primarily for assets that have a mid-term life, such as equipment or for amortizing working capital.

- ◆ Long-term debt, repayable over 10 to 30 years, is used for assets that have a long, useful life such as real estate and some forms of equipment.

On the basis of collateral, debt can be classified as:

- ◆ Unsecured debt that is offered by lenders to strong borrowers or by vendors in the form of trade credit.

- ◆ Debt secured by current assets, such as inventory and accounts receivable, that is used for working capital for growth.

- ◆ Debt secured by equipment.

- Debt secured by real estate.

- Debt secured by all the assets under the Uniform Commercial Code.

- Debt that is secured by all assets, but is subordinated to debt of institutional lenders, such as banks. This type of debt is offered by some types of venture capitalists, primarily small business investment companies or S.B.I.C.'s, and specialized S.B.I.C.'s, which are known as S.S.B.I.C.'s.

Trade credit, which is offered by vendors, is available to most established businesses and to many new businesses that the vendors judge to be viable. In most cases, there is no financing charge since the cost has been built in. Indeed, sometimes vendors offer very attractive discounts for payment of trade credit within 10 days or 15 days. It often pays to borrow money from a bank to take this discount, if you can obtain bank debt.

A form of financing called hybrid instruments combines features of debt and equity. Such instruments can include subordinated debt with convertibility features and warrants to buy stock. They are used in venture-capital-type transactions, when the company needs equity but the investors want interest on their debt, a better collateral position than common or preferred stockholders and repayment of principal, while obtaining a greater gain through an increase in the value of their warrants.

KEY 14

Use convertible instruments, warrants and options to your advantage

So-called hybrid instruments, which combine features of debt and equity, are useful in cases where the company needs equity financing but the investors want interest on their debt, a better collateral position than is available through ownership of common or preferred stock, repayment of principal and the potential for gain through an increase in the value of their warrants. These instruments can include:

◆ Subordinated convertible debt with or without detachable warrants. Many ventures need equity capital; banks won't lend them all the money they need because banks are not in the business of taking risk. If a business fails, the assets can usually never be sold for what the company paid to buy or build them. Therefore, the company needs to come up with the balance, in the form of equity.

Because obtaining equity from public

markets is not an option for many ventures, the only option available to their investors for realizing anticipated returns is to have their financial instruments redeemed by the company. While there are many laws regulating the circumstances under which companies can redeem stock, history shows that this strategy offers the lowest return to the investors.

Therefore, in these kinds of companies, sophisticated financiers would prefer to use subordinated convertible debt with detachable warrants. The debt feature allows them to have a set repayment schedule. The subordinated feature allows them to secure their loan and be senior to all unsecured creditors and equity. The convertible feature allows them to convert to common stock and share in the upside, if any. The detachable warrants allow them to buy stock in the company if the debt has been repaid. And the debt feature also offers an interest payment that provides them a return.

◆ Warrants. These allow the holder to buy a certain number of shares at a set price for a certain length of time. Warrants are usually used in conjunction with some other form of financial instrument, such as in a package with common or preferred stock to allow the investors to obtain more stock for an attractive price, or with subordinated debt as mentioned earlier. They are mainly used as "sweeteners" to nudge investors from the fence to the buyer category. And when (and if) investors exercise their warrants, the company gets more cash. So it pays to have an expiration date on the warrants in line with the company needs.

◆ Preferred stock. This can be attractive when the company does not have the cash flow to pay interest or principal on subordinated debt, and when the dividends can be cumulative but not payable for the first two or three years. The investors get the right to convert to common stock, and sophisticated investors prefer this because they usually ask for more rights than that available to common shareholders, they get paid before common shareholders and they can convert to common shares when the time is right.

Valuation of the above instruments can be quite complex and is more easily done when the company is large and publicly held. But if it is new and there is no history of payment and thus no reassurance of future payment, valuation is extremely tough and more of an art than a science.

In general, remember that the expected return to investors for the same venture and level of investment at any stage is highest if the instrument is common stock, with the total return being lower if the instrument is preferred stock and even lower if it is subordinated convertible debt.

And the interest rate paid on subordinated debt is higher than the dividend rate paid on preferred stock because interest costs are tax-deductible for the venture (hope springs eternal that the venture will one day be profitable and pay taxes) but dividends are not deductible.

KEY 15

Achieve the appropriate leverage, or mix between equity and debt, in the capital structure of your firm

Capital Structure includes both debt and equity that finances the assets of the firm. This mix is often described as leverage, meaning the amount of debt divided by the equity base, and typically measured by a "debt/equity" ratio. A debt/equity ratio of one means that the capital structure includes a dollar of debt for every dollar of equity. A ratio greater than one means more debt than equity; less than one, more equity than debt.

In a perfect world, a business would have a mix of debt and equity that minimized total cost of capital, dilution of owners' equity, and risk; and maximized control and flexibility. Because the world isn't perfect, business owners have to develop a mix appropriate for their businesses by making tradeoffs among cost, control, flexibility and dilution. The amount of leverage that lenders will provide, or that other equity holders will permit, may limit the ranges in which these tradeoffs can occur.

Most businesses minimize their cost of capital by having debt/equity ratios between 0.5 (50 cents of debt for every $1 of equity) and 2 ($2 of debt for every $1 of equity). To estimate an appropriate level for your business, check ratios for your industry in the annual guide published by Robert Morris Associates. Dun's also publishes industry ratios, as do other publishers. (Startup companies generally carry higher debt/equity ratios at the beginning, then move into the 0.5–2.0 range as they become established.)

Costs of capital are lower when you finance each type of asset with the appropriate funding: real estate and widely used equipment through debt or lease; specialized equipment and working capital through a combination of debt and equity, and product development through equity.

Each type of financing instrument has its own cost. In general, equity costs more than debt. Either equity, debt or a combination of the two will cost less from friends and family, and from development sources, than from professional investors or commercial sources.

Equity instruments are considered highest cost because investors demand a share of the company's earnings, and dividends paid are not tax-deductible. In addition, ownership given to investors results in a dilution of the entrepreneur's interest.

Equity investors typically require compounded annual returns in excess of 20 percent (see Key 12). Thus they will expect an investment of $1,000 to be worth more than $1,700 in three years. Investors will require higher returns for businesses that are very young or higher risk.

Money only means a lot when you aint got it.

Arthur Stringer, Weathered Oak

If other investors can find places to put their money at 20 percent or more in ventures of comparable risk, you should be sure that your own funds will earn that much in your venture. Unless you are seeking a lifestyle business, put your money elsewhere and take a job with a salary higher than most entrepreneurs can pay themselves. Recognize that profits retained in the business represent equity financing, and should generate commensurate returns when reinvested.

Sales of equity are typically more costly than placement of debt because fees for attorneys (and investment bankers) are higher for sale of equity. In addition, equity sales may require a professional appraisal to establish a value for the company. A valuation is necessary to determine the worth of the company as a whole, and therefore what percentage should be given up in exchange for a specified dollar investment.

If equity investors demand that the company be sold (so that they can cash in their stock) before the stock has reached its peak value, the entrepreneurs will receive less than they would have for their own stock and, if a controlling interest in the company is sold, may lose control of the company altogether.

Debt instruments have interest payments which are tax-deductible, but are payable whether the company is profitable or unprofitable, or has enough cash to pay the interest and required principal repayment. If the business cannot meet its payments, the lender may effectively close the business down. If the owners have personally guaranteed the loan, they could lose personal assets as well.

Interest rates may be fixed for the term of the loan, or variable. With fixed rates, lenders assume the risk of fluctuating interest rates. If rates go up, lenders cannot raise fixed rates; if rates go down, lenders will not give you a better deal. Variable rates transfer risks of fluctuating interest rates to the borrower, who pays more when rates go up; less, if they go down. You should get a fixed-rate loan if you can and the rate is reasonable. If you want to gamble on interest rates, you should be in the financial business. Unless you are, stick to the business you're in and don't try to out-guess the financiers. In the 1980's, many businesses that had taken variable-rate loans failed when interest rates approached 20 percent.

Total costs of debt include far more than the interest rate itself. Total costs include the points (percentages of the principal amount of the loan) and fees paid to the lender, as well as the legal and accounting fees the borrower will incur. Lenders may require that a borrower keep a minimum balance in an account—funds that the borrower pays for but cannot use. Loan covenants may force the borrower to incur costs or forgo opportunities. And don't forget the time you spend to obtain the loan—usually longer from development agencies than from commercial sources.

KEY 16

Carefully compare the various costs of financing

L ook at the total cost of each type of capital, including not just the interest rate and debt payments but also the considerations of dilution, risk, control, flexibility and reserves.

DILUTION

Dilution is the weakening effect that the exercise of options and warrants and the conversion of convertible securities have on the value of outstanding shares. You can minimize dilution by borrowing money instead of selling equity. But if you borrow too much, and lack the cash flow to repay the loans, you may lose the whole company. Some lenders may insist on having the option to convert their loans to stock, or may request warrants (options to buy stock on specified terms). In calculating dilution, you should compute the number of shares that financiers would own if they converted all their loan dollars to stock, and exercised all their warrants.

RETURN AND RISK

All things being equal, the lowest-cost capital

structure is the one that will yield the highest returns. Higher debt/equity ratios improve returns during profitable times, but can push the firm into insolvency during times when cash flow is tight. Companies with steady growth in cash flow may use their history and projections to justify higher levels of debt, but a firm with cyclical earnings and cash flows should not borrow more than it can repay during downswings. Some entrepreneurs are simply uncomfortable with "too much" debt, and are willing to forgo some return to reduce their risk of being unable to repay.

CONTROL

In general, if you borrow more, the lenders will have more control over your business.

The more equity you sell, the more control outside investors can exercise. Just as you want to diffuse control among equity holders (see Key 17), you may wish to use a mix of investors and lenders to avoid concentration of control. This strategy implies borrowing from multiple sources. If you do so, make sure that the covenants on the loans are consistent with one another, and that no one lender can restrict your actions. Recognize also that there is a cost to you of negotiating, and communicating continuously with, multiple investors and lenders.

FLEXIBILITY

Companies have more flexibility in their choice of funding when they have low debt/equity ratios, because they can take on debt or sell equity. Companies with high debt/equity ratios may have difficulty obtaining additional loans. If flexibility is important, keep a low debt/equity ratio. But recognize that this low ratio which provides the flexibility may be increasing your total cost of capital over the minimum it could be. There is a cost to flexibility.

RESERVES

Don't try to fine-tune your capital structure beyond what you know and can anticipate.

No forecast is perfect, and investors and lenders are more concerned with their return and risk profiles than with fine-tuning your capital structure. Build into your structure some financial reserves for unanticipated setbacks or opportunities. Financiers and suppliers can become quite unfriendly when you have to seek extended terms or additional financing because initial plans provided no reserves for the unexpected.

Few fiduciaries have any mental fun while they fiduce.

Robert Kirk Miller

KEY 17

To grow, you may have to control via performance. But don't let contol concentrate

---

The way you finance your business will affect your control over it. Raising equity is easier if you seek control through performance rather than stock.

To keep 100 percent control over your business:

◆ sell no stock to anyone else;

◆ borrow no money;

◆ hire no key employees whose departure would hurt the business;

◆ employ no resources (such as technology, components and trade names) whose use is restricted.

If you demand complete control, your business will likely remain insignificant and have limited flexibility to adapt to changing circumstances—and its chances of failure will be greater.

So if you intend to build a substantial business, the question becomes how to finance it to balance control, flexibility and growth.

If you sell equity worth less than half your business, and the investors impose no covenants, you retain shareholder control. You own more than half of the common voting shares of the company, and are not encumbered by any agreements on how you can vote them. You can elect a majority of board members (sometimes all of them), and decide the future direction of the company, including deployment of assets and the size and components of compensation.

If you sell any equity to professional investors or venture capitalists, they will demand strategic control, giving them the right to hold seats on the board of directors, veto changes in strategic direction (they won't want you to build a hotel in the Bahamas if you said you planned to start a high-tech company in Louisville) and set executive compensation (which they will do with an emphasis on awarding options to buy stock in the future rather than paying high salaries that take cash from the company now).

Both the amount of stock you sell and the people you sell it to can affect your sway over the company. One way to maximize your influence is to maintain control over the board of directors. Instead of selling equity to only one investor, sell it to many, some of whom will take a less than active role on the board. If possible, retain for yourself a bloc of shares larger than that of any other single investor. In such a situation, three or four investors representing more than half the company's stock would have to join together to force changes in the strategic direction of the company, or to oust you as chief executive.

You can keep effective control of the business by performing effectively, persuading the other key players by the force of your argument and results, and maintaining continuous communication with them.

The key is to avoid giving more than half the company to a single investor, because you will likely lose the company and that investor will walk away with the lion's share of the profits and higher stock price.

You may want key employees—individuals without whom the business would be seriously impaired—to hold stock for two reasons. First, they will almost always vote with you. Second, their stock can work like "golden handcuffs" to retain employees because it is usually subject to a buy-back agreement if they leave the firm.

Ask yourself whether you would rather be the owner of the next eBay—the Internet auctioneer whose market value soared more than 1,000 percent to $22 billion in less than a year—even if it means the risk of losing the business if you don't play your cards right, or the owner of the next Zauction, which went under because the owners insisted on retaining control instead of raising the equity capital that would allow them to grow and compete.

Investors will be wary of agreements restricting your use of critical resources, lest those agreements limit your ability to grow and adapt (and thus increase the value of the company). Avoid, if you can, restrictive covenants on technology, trade names, proprietary information or other intellectual property and restrictions on reselling purchased components or products.

KEY 18

Save your equity to use for working capital and development expenses

L enders are more likely to lend against "hard" assets than against current assets. When bankers make a loan, they prefer collateral that can be easily liquidated in the event of a foreclosure; thus, they want to know the availability of the asset, its liquidation value and the ease with which it can be sold off.

Based on their availability upon foreclosure, fixed assets, such as real estate and equipment, are preferable to inventory. This is because real estate and equipment (especially equipment without wheels) usually do not disappear when the company is in trouble. Inventory is sometimes apt to vanish when the lenders go to collect the assets after foreclosure.

Even if all the assets are still on the premises, fixed assets are normally easier to liquidate (sell or lease to someone else) than inventory. This allows the lenders to obtain their funds sooner. Also, real estate and general-purpose equipment maintain their value better than inventory and can be liquidated at higher values, especially during inflationary times.

Even development financiers (local, state and federal programs to develop poor geographic areas or help certain kinds of entrepreneurs) prefer fixed assets. Many development financiers are not as well trained as financiers and financing against current assets (inventory, accounts receivable) requires greater skill and expertise.

Accounts receivable from credit-worthy customers are usually more desirable than inventory. But even here, lenders have found that it is often difficult for them to collect past-due receivables from customers if the borrower has gone out of business.

In sum, working capital financing, whether from lenders such as commercial-finance companies or from investors as equity, is usually more expensive than fixed-asset financing. To reduce the cost of financing to the firm, save your limited capital and think twice before investing your scarce cash in real estate.

Some assets are easier to finance than others. You should probably lease real estate if you have limited cash or if you are a startup. Ask yourself whether you are in the real-estate business or in some other business before you invest in real estate for capital gains. If you are committed to buy and own real estate, use attractive development-finance programs such as tax-increment financing (if available) and high-leverage programs, such as the S.B.A.'s 504 program, to conserve cash for working capital.

Due to the tax benefits of owning real estate and

other factors, many rich investors would prefer to buy and lease out real estate.

Likewise, many investors will lease you equipment that they own as a fixed asset that can be depreciated. So when you are not cash rich, lease equipment. And if you have to own, use local, state and federal development finance programs.

Any jackass can draw up a balanced budget on paper.

Lane Kirkland, **U.S. News and World Report**

KEY 19

When raising equity, value your business as fairly and accurately as you can

In venture-capital-type deals, valuation of the company is very important because it influences the amounts of equity given up. Equally important, many investors won't even consider a potential investment if the valuation is sky-high.

We have known a few ventures that either failed or never reached their potential because the entrepreneurs put valuations on them that could not be "sold" to professionals—and thus they failed to raise the financing they needed.

This can often happen when you have raised financing from your friends and family at valuations that are not realistic. And now you don't want to give them the impression that you either didn't know what you were doing or else exploited them. But that may be what you have to do to raise money from professionals, who are able to assess your venture's potential better than your family or even you can.

In evaluating a value on their business, many entrepreneurs let their emotions take over and factor in all the sweat and tears, and money, they have put into it. Investors, however, look cold-bloodedly at the current stage of the business and its prospects for creating wealth and value.

You should too. Skip the nostalgia and act as though somebody else owns your business and ask whether you would plunk your hard-earned cash into it. Better yet, pretend the money is your mother's nest egg and that she needs a decent return for her retirement.

This assumes that you know how professional venture capitalists arrive at their valuations. What do they look at? They don't care that much that you spent 10 years developing your product or service. What they are interested in is the value of what you have developed. If you have discovered a formula to convert lead to gold economically, they will value it highly. If your product can be copied by someone else easily, they will not value it highly. If it has a sales potential of $100 million, they will value it highly. If the potential is $1 million, they will not value it highly.

Don't quibble about small percentages when someone offers you the money you want. Save your negotiating energy for the important battles. In fact, unless you truly believe that a professional investor's valuation is unreasonable, you should probably accept it. Although valuation is more an art than a science, and no two investors are likely to arrive at the same number if they do independent valuations, professionals have a system behind their seeming madness. Ask the venture capitalists how they arrived at their valuation.

Sometimes you might find out that they valued

your business lower than you expected because they do not believe your projections. Although most entrepreneurs will claim their projections are "conservative," the investors take this contention with a huge grain of salt. (I myself have looked at hundreds of businesses over the years, and without exception was told by the owners that their projections were conservative. Yet, in 99 percent of the cases, they were vastly overblown.)

What do you do if you really, truly believe you can meet your projections? Negotiate for an "earn out." This means that you'll keep more of the venture if you achieve your projections, or do better. But the investors will get more of the venture to earn the return they expect if you do not.

Traditional valuation methods may not fit the startup situation for different reasons:

- ◆ "Current net worth" (book value) has limited meaning for most startups, because current book value substantially understates the future earning power of the firm.

- ◆ "Multiple of cash flow" is meaningless in most high-growth ventures that don't have positive cash flow.

- ◆ "Current actual market value" is inappropriate because most high-growth ventures don't have a public market for their stock to obtain a fair market value.

- ◆ "Current market value based on multiples" (such as price-to-earnings or cash-flow ratios) of similar companies can be useful only if your business is "similar" or "comparable" to some other set of firms whose values are known. If a new venture has

negligible cash flow or profit, multiples—
whether based on "comparable" firms or
not—may be meaningless.

◆ "Present value of future market valuation"
is the most frequently used method. The
problem for entrepreneurs occurs when the
venture capitalists do not believe the projections, or want a higher return than the
entrepreneurs think is appropriate given the
venture's stage and prospects.

KEY 20

Read the covenants on financing agreements. All clauses obtain flexibility

Covenants are agreements that you sign upon obtaining a loan or investment. They can include positive covenants and negative covenants.

Positive covenants specify actions that you will take, such as maintaining a certain level of insurance and developing monthly financial statements and sending a copy to the lender.

Negative covenants are clauses that keep you from doing things that can injure the financier. These describe actions that you cannot take, like paying yourself a high salary or high dividends and selling key assets or portions of your business.

Financial covenants spell out financial ratios and numbers that you must maintain; you should examine these stipulations with special care. The numbers can include net worth and the levels of receivables and inventory and the ratios can include equity to assets, operating income to interest payment and total cash flow to principal.

Debt instruments may carry more onerous covenants, causing some entrepreneurs to opt for more equity. Debt instruments also usually restrict flexibility more than equity, thus increasing the risk of default.

You should study the covenants to determine which terms you can live with and which ones you cannot. You should then negotiate with the financiers about modifying those that pose a problem. Most financiers are open to such negotiation, because they want to be sure that you can live up to the agreements.

Naturally, you should move heaven and earth to do so. But realistically, there is always the chance you will fall short of one or more goals, and you should seek out financiers who will be willing to renegotiate the numbers. Banks and other institutions that specialize in your industry or geographic area often show such flexibility because they want to maintain their market leadership. An added bonus is that they know the problems you face and can help solve them.

In an equity financing, you can lose control of your company if you don't satisfy your covenants. Some equity agreements allow you to run the company only so long as the company is meeting its projections and milestones. Any serious breach can result in the financiers' taking control of the board of directors and changing the management team—including you.

KEY 21

Don't gamble with fluctuating interest rates. Lock them up if they're reasonable and you can make a profit

Would you rather have certain, but perhaps slightly smaller, profits? Or would you prefer to gamble your company on uncertain, and highly fluctuating, profits?

If you choose the latter, you should not start a business. You should take whatever money you were going to invest in your business, gamble it on interest-rate futures, go broke and then find a job.

If you disagree, you might want to examine the savings and loan debacle of the 1980s. While greed, graft and cronyism, as well as the Government's unbelievable laissez-faire policies, all contributed to the debacle, the widespread practice by S&L's of making long-term loans at fixed rates while borrowing on short-term notes sealed the fate of many. When short-term rates rose wildly, they were doomed.

If that can happen to financial institutions, why do you think it can't happen to you?

The best strategy is to seek fixed rates on long-term notes for such purposes as financing real estate and equipment and variable rates on short-term notes used for building current assets. That way, if the short-term credit gets too expensive, you can merely reduce the level of your business and its assets and pay down the loan. You'd have a lot more trouble unloading your building or equipment—an expensive proposition in any case—so you should protect yourself with fixed rates to finance them.

Where can you find fixed-rate loans?

One of the best government programs available is the Small Business Administration's so-called 504 loans. These loans are fixed for 10 years (when your loan requirements are predominantly for equipment with long lives) or for 20 years (when your loan requirements are for real estate). While there is some cost and truly hellish paperwork, especially for closing the loan (invented, we are convinced, by a sadist), the interest rates are based on the United States Treasury Bond rates for the time period.

Who else in their right minds would give you—a small business—fixed rate loans for 10 years or 20 years at rates close to the best borrower in the world?

And the S.B.A. has another goodie called the S.B.A. 7(a) program, which guarantees about 80 percent of a fixed-rate loan from a bank or other institutional lender. The guaranteed portion can be sold on the secondary markets by the lenders at rates close to United States Treasury bond rates. Unless you ask your lenders about this provision, they may not bring it up because otherwise they may have to pass on the savings to you. (For a list of brokers who can help place the guaranteed portion, call the S.B.A.'s 1-800 number or visit their web site (www.sba.gov).

KEY 22

Prove the ability of the business to generate positive income—and cash flow before reinvestment—as promptly as possible

D o not squander cash on frills. Temporal sins are synonymous with worldly pleasures and the promise of punishment in the hereafter. Financial sins are different. They usually carry a hefty penalty in this world.

Cash is king when you are trying to raise money. Do not squander your cash on expenses that are not absolutely necessary, and especially avoid wasting it on ego gratification, like renting posh quarters; on "employee fulfillment" programs when you haven't even made a penny in profit, or on toys such as airplanes.

Treat your cash as gold—it is that valuable. Use it to cross the first two hurdles of any startup: proving to lenders and investors that you can actually achieve sales at prices that offer a decent gross margin, and proving that you can actually make an after-tax profit and thus that you have the potential for growth.

Businesses that are growing at a rapid pace need to reinvest in the company constantly to sustain the growth. Alas, many fail to raise the necessary money from lenders and investors on the erroneous assumption that they can eventually get financing from their vendors, employees or even Uncle Sam (in the form of withholdings).

Vendors will extend you credit, but they want to be repaid on their terms. Employees are not working for you to finance you. And Uncle Sam hates to finance businesses without knowing about it.

Many high-tech companies have disappeared into bankruptcy because they used their working capital and their profits to buy or rent expensive real estate to show off their temporary success. In the meantime, their competitors invested in more advanced technology. Guess who won?

Don't waste equity financing that you have raised at an annualized cost (based on dilution—the opportunity cost you have given up) in excess of 20 percent, or debt that you have personally guaranteed. Don't delude yourself into thinking that thick carpets, luxury offices and airplanes are needed to succeed in business when you were previously managing very well without them. Ask yourself whether the investment in your ego is worth paying someone the high cost of money.

When starting your business, you often have the choice of "make versus buy." This means that you can invest in fixed assets, that is, "make it yourself," or have someone else make it for you.

If it does not mean giving away the crown jewels, minimize your fixed costs and have someone else make it for you. Achieve breakeven status (i.e., show a profit) as soon as possible. Keep in mind that in some fields, such as the Internet, you may have to invest heavily in marketing to establish a presence. America Online did this, and look where it is now. So don't be dogmatic about hewing to this rule.

If cash comes with fame, come fame. If cash comes without fame, come cash.

Jack London

KEY 23

Monitor your actual perform-ance against your assumptions. You might need more cash, or need it sooner

The first step in monitoring is to understand your projections. That requires you either to do your own projections or to take an active role when your accountant or consultant does them. Asking a specialist to do the calculations makes sense, but if you, the leader of the company, fail to get deeply involved in every aspect of the analysis, you won't understand what makes your business tick. Sooner or later, you will pay a heavy price for your ignorance, unless you have hired a great chief financial officer who will tell you when you are stumbling. Moreover, by taking part in the process, you will be in a position to seize opportunities and avoid problems you might not otherwise have spotted.

To do a great job of monitoring your performance, you need to do your projections on a "bottom up" basis (see Key 2.). This throws a spotlight on the foundation blocks upon which you have built your business. If you have assumed, for example, that you will make sales averaging $20 (or

I cried all the way to
the bank.

Liberace, An Autobiography

$20,000) per customer, and the average is only half that, your actual performance will obviously differ quite markedly from your projected performance. Even if you offset the deficiency in revenues by drumming up twice as many customers as you projected, you will probably discover that you had to spend a lot more on marketing and service than you planned.

How frequently should you monitor your performance? The general rule is: Often, and quickly. A quarterly review is better than an annual review; a monthly review is better still, and a weekly review is best of all—it lets you identify and react to your strengths and weaknesses more quickly. Having been involved in a number of turnarounds, I have found that getting accurate statements and getting them more frequently is crucial to figuring out what is going wrong and what is going right, and that sharing the information with the managers so that they can improve the performance of their departments is crucial to nursing the business back to health.

In addition, the more quickly you monitor your business, the better off you'll be. If you get monthly statements 25 days after the end of the month, you will only be able to take corrective action 55 days away from the start of the month in which the problem popped up. When you try to solve the problem, your managers might well tell you that you are reacting to old news and that you need to turn your attention to what is happening now.

On the other hand, if on a Monday morning you are able to compare your earlier projections with what actually happened the previous week, you can discuss your operations with your key employees when their memory is fresh and take action before another 48 days have elapsed.

You need to monitor the key variables in your business. On a weekly or daily basis (and yes, I have on occasion asked for daily progress reports), these include the levels of sales, collections, cash, payables, receivables, and cost of materials and labor. On a monthly basis, you should also examine your overhead figures and break-even levels.

Accuracy is absolutely essential, and make sure your accountants understand that. However, you need to understand when you can live with close approximations. Your accountant will fight you when you ask for weekly or daily statements, since some of the monthly expenses will not be known until the end of the month. Fine; ask them to give you their best approximations, and then make corrections at the end of the month.

Ask yourself: Whom are you fooling if you "cook"

your statements? Many entrepreneurs believe that they can fool their bankers by giving them over-optimistic statements to get the loan. But if you have not addressed the key problems, you are only digging a deeper hole for yourself.

Whom do you compare yourself against? Your peers. And their figures are available from a number of sources, such as the Dun & Bradstreet Corporation, a distributor of financial information, or Robert Morris Associates, a trade group for commercial lenders. Talk to your information specialist (they used to be called librarians!) at the largest public or university library near you. They might charge a small fee for special help, but it will be worth it.

Remember: It is better to have simple, easily understood and accurate statements than statements that only your accountant could love.

KEY 24

Keep financiers informed about your progress or problems. Do not wait till the last minute, especially with bad news

Many entrepreneurs think that keeping bad news to themselves will give them time to straighten out the mess.

Financiers know there is something wrong when financial statements arrive late or not at all. And this is when they start to feel queasy about your loan.

All financiers have clauses in their contract about the timely submission of accurate financial statements. When you violate this clause, they think that you are trying to hide something, and so they are more likely to call the loan.

Lenders and investors are more likely to be lenient if they are informed immediately about a problem and told what is being done to correct it. Get your financiers involved in developing the solution. Often, they will work with you or refer you to people who can help.

Financiers hate surprises, especially when they

are the last to know. This is often when they pull the rug out from under the entrepreneurs.

When tackling your problems, keep in mind that money alone will not solve everything. I have seen many companies that were mismanaged (a broad term that can include just about anything you can think of) but that needed to correct sloppy thinking or counterproductive behavior every bit as much as they needed to raise more capital. Sometimes, an infusion of cash alone only prolongs the company's agony.

In such cases, it is important that you obtain good, impartial and non-emotional advice to determine your course of action.

Talk to your financiers even when times are good. There have been a number of companies that have failed when their sales exceeded their expectations. This is because higher sales often require larger inventories and greater levels of accounts receivable—which leads to the need for more financing. If you don't raise this in time, you end up relying on reluctant or unwitting financiers like your vendors or Uncle Sam.

Also, talk to your financiers before making strategic changes. You are probably required to anyway by your financing agreement, but even if you aren't, they won't be happy if you sell a major division without informing them first.

If you are ever in doubt whether you are providing too much information to your financiers, ask them. I have never known a financier to say that they received too much information, though some complain about the lack of a summary or analysis of large volumes of data.

KEY 25

Your planning for future financing is never done

N o matter what type of business you run—whether a family retail shop, a fast-growth technology company or a mid-sized manufacturer—you should constantly be making plans for future financing.

Why? Because things might be rosy today, but cloudy tomorrow. Or you might be introduced to a new opportunity, such as the acquisition of your principal competitor; if you haven't kept some financial powder dry, you might watch in distress as another competitor buys him out.

More prosaically, you might simply need a bit of extra cash to cope with the inevitable changes in the business environment.

The key factor to consider in evaluating your future financing is your financial structure, that is, the levels of your debt and equity. While you might have settled on a supposedly ideal balance between the two, you shouldn't be dogmatic about it. Let circumstances and common sense, not some preconceived notion, dictate the mix.

For example, when the equity markets are on a rampage (as they were in the late 1990s), you might want to raise additional equity if you can do so, even though you don't need it right away. This is exactly what many Internet companies, including e-Bay, did. Seeing how well their initial public offerings were accepted and how high their companies were valued, they went right back to the markets and raised additional funds by selling additional stock. Their thinking might well have been, "Who knows when the good times will stop rolling? Let's build a war chest now."

By the same token, it might make eminent sense for some companies to increase their long-term, fixed-rate debt, even if they have no pressing need for money. As of mid-1999, for example, long-term rates had not been lower for decades, and a lot of entrepreneurs took out loans to lock them in. You might have to pay a penalty if you prepay them, but at least you will have the peace of mind of knowing that you are sitting pretty if rates suddenly shoot up.

Always have some borrowing capacity available. If you err, err on the side of having a little more equity than your ideal structure provides for (assuming that it is possible for your company to raise a little more equity without suffering high dilution). Then, when you are faced with either an emergency or opportunity and need cash, you will have reserves to tap.

As you grow and become more profitable, more sophisticated financiers will be calling on you to sell their wares. Grab the chance while the sun is shining; if storm clouds appear, they'll make themselves scarce.

Which brings up one final point: Remember the financiers who helped you when your venture was young and struggling. Stick by them; when tough times return, they will most likely stick by you.

Seest thou a man diligent at his business? He shall stand before kings, he shall not stand before mean men.

Old Testament, **Proverbs**

INDEX

AUTHORS

DILEEP RAO, Ph.D., is an Adjunct Professor of Entrepreneurial Studies, Business Planning, and Venture Finance at the Carlson School of Management at the University of Minnesota. He has financed hundreds of emerging ventures and growing businesses as a venture capitalist, leader and investment banker. Currently, he is president of Inter-Finance Corporation, a consultant on business, financial, and development strategy to emerging ventures and growing businesses, financial institutions, and economic development agencies, and is the author of 5 reference books for emerging businesses, including the *Handbook of Business Finance & Capital Sources*.

RICHARD N. CARDOZO holds the Carlson Chair in Entrepreneurial Studies and is Professor of Marketing in the Carlson School of Management at the University of Minnesota. His teaching and research activities focus on the formation and growth of independent business firms and internal corporate ventures. He has special interest in emerging businesses in industrial markets. He has written numerous books and articles on entrepreneurship, new product marketing and industrial marketing and has served on the editorial boards of the *Journal of Business Venturing*, the *Journal of Marketing* and the *Journal of Marketing Research*. Professor Cardozo has served as a director of Best Buy Company, the Valspar Corporation and National Presto Industries, and as a consultant to growing corporations.